Memorable Musings and Meditations 1.5

Kyle Ohree

BookLeaf Publishing

India | USA | UK

Memorable Musings and Meditations 1.5 ©
2024 Kyle Ohree

Presentation by *BookLeaf Publishing*

Web: www.bookleafpub.com

E-mail: info@bookleafpub.com

ISBN: 9789360944285

First edition 2024

For all those that touched my soul and aren't around today:

Brian Mackey, Phillip Galbmilion, Ricardo Ramjattan, Aunty Glenda, Grandma Lucienne, Grandma Hilda, and Grandpa Sims.

ACKNOWLEDGEMENT

To my firstborn, MAKO and my second born, Ky-Raah. Daddy love you both immeasurably. You both inspire me daily.

To my wife, thanks for always pushing me to grander heights.

Sunset

My brown eyes are set
Ablaze by such fiery skies
Adoring the oranges and lush pinks descending
upon our gazes,
To be marvelled at in their evolution.

For the transitions to bloom,
The arrays of brilliance of our benevolent Sun
Must slowly vanish,
Beneath the horizon.
This begins the colorful displays.

With blues and yellows like flowery fields,
Becoming warm oranges caressing the soul,
To soft pink wisps of cloud delectable as cotton
candy lightly graces the tongue.
My eyes are overjoyed.

Water

You think me insignificant,
a single drop of rain.
But when we all come together,
we cause hurricanes.
A single drop can do no harm,
but never underestimate the
ferocity of a typhoon.
I bring life and destruction, I'm
bittersweet.
The relief you need on a
hot summer's day.
The crisp dew blanketing the
Earth early in the morning.

Soothing your very soul,
yet capable of tearing asunder
all you cherish.
Fear me, loathe me,
love me, worship me:
I am creation and destruction.
But most of all,
I am life itself.

Crash into me, like I do the
rocky shore.

Let me fill up your lungs,
take your breath away
like a tight hug from a loved
one.
For a single drop cannot do
much,
but together we take what we desire.

Kind

As the orange rays eminante from the horizon,
such warmth radiates within
my very soul.
transfornative in rearranging my very essence.

Beneath such sullen eyes
lies joy waiting to be unearthed.
your sugary words and gestures
can crack such a hardened shell.

so bring forth your endless bounty,
of generosity to wash
over me with warming waters,
eroding away my endless sorrows.

2022/02/14

5

Memories can not replace
Love displaced by time,
Feelings can't be unfelt,
Unsent like IG messages.

Feelings cannot convey
Love everlasting.
But those bonds, once severed
Become a catastrophe.

But yet we pursue
Love anew, revitalized by
Daylight's early glow,
Your horizon I wish to cross
And set forth on a sunnier day.

SMS

Messages delivered
by instant speech,
delivering a full spectrum of emotions.

my heart overflows
as these same syllables
elicit joy and sorrow immeasurable.

sing your sweet lyrics
directly to my soul
build me up better than yesterday.

Honey

Melting juices oozing
such pleasurable sweetness
through the entirety of my tongue.

my senses overload with
joys once held unknown
to my life.

as I take another
spoonful, my heart and soul
erupt once more.

Eclectic

Zigs and zags of electric
Yellows and blues
Exotically coloring tropical patterns
Within a light shirt.

Her eyes, ablaze with flames
Inextinguishable and scalding.
Such spirit cannot be contained
By ordinary expression.

Separately, each item is
Uniquely defined.
But pulled together by an indomitable will,
They form a mosaic far beyond beautiful.

Compassion

A myriad of colors
Exuded from a visible aura,
Of a beloved hero.

With soothing eyes as
Frosted touches meet burning skin.
The fires of such love
Permeate through the toughest shells.

If only more could exude
Such stunning displays
This world would be
Truly bright.

Stargazing

As I lay back, reclining
On the deserted ground.
A dazzling array of stars
Shooting across the darkened sky,
Illuminates my blackened eyes.

Such a dazzling display,
Cannot be conveyed
In mere words.
The celestial bodies
Dancings so brightly
As they spell out incredible
Imagery.

I lay speechless,
Marvelling at such beauty.
My soul refreshed,
I stand up to take in
Further picturesque pieces
Of raw artistic beauty in light.

Senses

Warmth, as the fireside
Flickers brilliantly orange,
Exuded in all you do.

Benevolence in your aura,
As overwhelmingly pleasant
As scents of eucalyptus.

Strive to press forth
And deliver your warmth
To the cold and weary.

Insidious

Singular steps reverberate through
The halls of madness slowly
Engulfing my soul.

An innocuous bite,
Leaving only two indentations
Slowly led to my demise.

Sanity is subjective,
A spectrum consisting of
Where I was and where I am now.

My future state is even more
Grave.
And my mind cannot convey the
Ramblings which spill forth
Quickly enough to save
What's left of me.

Peace

Tranquil waters cascading
Cooling revitalizing elixirs
Directly into my consciousness.

Your presence is serenity,
Personified in leaves floating,
Caressed by gentle breezes
And the slight humming of
Birds in the distance.

My soul rests so
Soundly, as trees
Rest in the forest after falling.

Not a morbid finality,
But a true ambiance of freedom
From all the evils of this world.

The slight caresses and soothing waters
Turn a tortured soul into
Angelic dreams of true restfulness,
A utopia in this reality.

Vertigo

Gazing out across
The landscape from
Overlooking from the balcony' edge.

My eyes cannot
Overlook such beauty immaculately
Populating my vision.

As I stare down,
My stomach leaps,
Bounds over and again at
Such a dramatic fall.

So distant, this cityscape from
My lookout position,
Sickened by the height,
But in awe of the city's lights.

Sonnet

Gazing upon your brilliant aura,
All eyes grow weary with joy unbridled.
Vividly projecting colors of flora,
Violets, Roses, a bouquet unrivaled.

Words truly cannot describe such a gem,
Naturally made into a glowing form.
To provide us all with light through mayhem,
And comforting warmth when we're forlorn.

Our hearts despair forever, with longing
For grander visions of life picturesque.
As blackened nights lead towards the dawning
Of brilliant beauty, made from the grotesque.

Captivating, capturing our sullen souls
Emancipating, emanating Jubilance: sanctifying
my ailments.

Tender Love

Not just succulent
Kisses in the morning
To begin a beautiful day,
But the tender caresses
We long for always.

Between long hours
Of strife and toil,
Our love can only
Simmer then boil.

Such a longing, seeking
Validation in
Silent glances,
Stares into spaces of
One another's irises.

Our state of being
Can only be described
As tenderness surviving.

Bubbling Over

Filling up so
Joyously with fluttering
Feelings washing over my face
With revitalizing refreshment.

Gazing upon,
Your smile provides
The light with which my
Heart can be guided
Back to a warm embrace.

My soul simply steams
With burning passions
For yours,
A soul so pure,
Causing my being
To transcend beyond physical
Shells detaining us from
Eternal Jubilation.

Endless Void

As nighttime falls,
Descending sorrows
Follow me like
Vultures to a carcass.

My spirit is devoid
Of sparks which seek
To cast everlasting light
Across my skies.

So I continue to
Seek such a
Fixture of light,
Controlled not by a switch,
But will illuminate
This empty Universe.

Blister

One bad blister
On my toe
Bringing me
Great turmoil and woe.

My anguish upon
My delectable skin,
Lies where
My foot begins.

I cannot despair,
For there's much to do
But my pain is immense,
And despair is true.

Vessel

With weary hands,
Trembling cold without
Your radiance beside to
Make bearable such
Lonely days.

I've begun anew.
Cold.
Resentful.
Starkly contrasting my
Previous existence,
My very essence.

If there's no Moon
To pull my heart's
Tides, to ebb and flow
Along with your
Sinful glances
And angelic smirks.

Nor if there's
No Sun to
Brighten and warm,
Refresh my soul,
Revitalizing and cleansing

My essence towards
Reaching Nirvana.

Then what is left?

But an empty shell,
Decrepit and still
Moving forward towards
Something still perceived
As beauty defined.

Starlight

Flickers of brilliance,
Burning away from
Such a benevolent core.
With heat and light
Radiating throughout the cosmos.

If I could only
Behold your
Magnificence again,
From millions of years ago,
As your celestial form
Now reaches my eyes.
I pray to have
A million more to
Behold your
Magnificence ever more.

SuperMoon

Glowing with supernatural
Light radiating forth
Waves of emotional
Instability,
Yet majestically
Gorgeous to behold.

This Moon shall
Forever sway me,
With its ebbs,
Flows,
Gravitational pulls
Of my emotional tides
To recede and flood.

I cannot resist its
Allures.
Too powerful are
Its seductive glances.
My heart responds
Involuntarily with
Great obedience and
My body merely follows.

Ebbs

And
Flows,
Cause my emotions
To recede,
To overflow,
I'm left here
Devoid of reason.
Until the Moon's
Power dissipates
Once more.